Safari Animals™
Animales de safari™

LIONS
LEONES

Amelie von Zumbusch

Traducción al español: Ma. Pilar Sanz

PowerKiDS press™ & **Editorial Buenas Letras™**

New York

Published in 2007 by The Rosen Publishing Group, Inc.
29 East 21st Street, New York, NY 10010

Copyright © 2007 by The Rosen Publishing Group, Inc.

First Edition

Book Design: Erica Clendening
Layout Design: Julio Gil and Lissette González

Photo Credits: Cover, pp. 1, 5, 9, 11, 13, 15, 21, 24 (top left, top right, bottom right) © Digital Vision; p. 7, 24 (bottom left) © Digital Stock; pp. 17, 19, 23 © Artville.

Cataloging Data

Zumbusch, Amelie von.
Lions-Leones / Amelie von Zumbusch; traducción al español: Ma. Pilar Sanz — 1st ed.
    p. cm. —   (Safari animals-Animales de safari)
Includes index.
ISBN-13: 978-1-4042-7608-6 (library binding)
ISBN-10: 1-4042-7608-4 (library binding)
1. Lions—Juvenile literature. 2. Spanish Language Materials I. Title.

Manufactured in the United States of America

CONTENTS

CONTENIDO

Lions are members of the cat family. They are big and strong.

Los leones pertenecen a la familia de los gatos. Los leones son grandes y fuertes.

Lions live in Africa. Most lions live on the grassy savannah.

Los leones viven en África. La mayoría de los leones viven en las hierbas de la sabana.

Male lions have a mane of hair around their face.

Los leones macho tienen una melena de pelo alrededor de la cara.

A group of lions is called a pride. The members of a pride work together.

Un grupo de leones se llama manada. Los leones de una manada trabajan en equipo.

Mother lions have from two to four babies at a time. Baby lions are called cubs.

Las leonas mamá tienen dos o tres bebés al mismo tiempo. A los bebés de león se les llama cachorros.

Lion cubs like to chase each other. They also like to climb trees.

A los cachorros de león les gusta perseguirse los unos a los otros. También les gusta trepar a los árboles.

Lions eat meat. They track other animals for food.

Los leones comen carne. Los leones persiguen a otros animales para conseguir su comida.

Lions have big teeth. They use these teeth to catch their food.

Los leones tienen dientes muy grandes. Los leones usan los dientes para atrapar a sus presas.

Lions need water as well as food. They lap water up with their tongues.

Los leones necesitan agua y comida. Los leones usan sus lenguas para tomar agua.

Lions spend much of the day napping. Sometimes they sleep in trees.

Los leones pasan mucho tiempo durmiendo la siesta. En ocasiones duermen en los árboles.

Words to Know / Palabras que debes saber

mane / (la) melena

pride / (la) manada

savannah / (la) sabana

tongue / (la) lengua